W9-BMG-907

The Outer Banks

An historical adventure
from Kitty Hawk to
Ocracoke

Martin R. Conway

Edited and Designed
by
Susan Knott

Carabelle Books
Box 1611
Shepherdstown, WV 25443
Copyright© 1984 by Carabelle Books
ALL RIGHTS RESERVED
Library of Congress Catalog Number: 84-71012
1SBN 0-938634-05-4

Printed in the United States
of America
Special Edition

Library of Congress Cataloging in Publication Data

Conway, Martin, 1928-
  The Outer Banks.

  Expanded ed. of: Outer Banks. Reston, Va. : Carabelle Books, 1983, 2nd ed.
  Bibliography: p.82
  Includes index.
  1. Outer Banks (N.C.) — History, Local. 2. Outer Banks
(N.C.) — Description and travel — Guide-books. I. Title.
F262.096096 1984   975.6'1   84-9536
ISBN 0-938634-05-4 (alk. paper)

CONTENTS

St. Andrew's by the Sea was built in 1849 by the summer residents of Old Nags Head. During the Civil War the Union forces demolished the church and used the lumber for shelters for fugitive slaves. Following the war the congregation petitioned the United States Government and eventually received compensation for their losses. St. Andrew's was rebuilt in 1915; it was moved, however, in 1937 from the sound side to where it stands today amid the dunes by the sea.

A Place Apart

There are few places in the United States that can match the Outer Banks of North Carolina for its rich diversity of historic events and appealing recreational attractions. Geographically, culturally and historically, the Outer Banks offers much enrichment to visitors.

It is the purpose of this book to help you discover the historic highlights, as well as a few of the natural wonders, of this fascinating place. History is deeply etched in the sands of this coastal region where from the village of Kitty Hawk to the isle of Ocracoke, you will find many a silent setting of dramatic events in the nation's past.

This book covers approximately 90 miles — from Kitty Hawk to Ocracoke — of the 175 miles that comprise the Outer Banks. Although Roanoke Island is not technically part of the Outer Banks, the histories of both are so interwoven that in any written account of their past, it would be impossible to include one without the other.

The most enduring legacy of Indian civilization on the Outer Banks is the retention of Indian names. Note, as you travel the Banks, these delightful remembrances of a day past: Kitty Hawk, Hatteras, Roanoke, Croatan, Pamilico, Ocracoke, Kinnakeet, Chicamacomico, Manteo, and Wanchese.

To appreciate the Outer Banks, it is important to leave the beaten paths and to explore the byways that offer surprise, delight and charm. Park your vehicle frequently and explore on foot. Above all, talk with the natives — a proud and distinguished people who have much to tell about things of the sea and of life.

This historical adventure can be completed in a day, but to get the most from your visit, the Banks must be savored unhurriedly. Begin early and stop frequently. A visit to the Outer Banks would be incomplete without taking the refreshing 40-minute (14 mile) ferry ride across Hatteras Inlet. And it is *Free* — courtesy of the state of North Carolina.

It is our hope that this book will help create an awareness of time passed at this special place, and that with this new awareness your visit will be even more exciting and meaningful. ENJOY!

Kitty Hawk Village has changed from the days when Wilbur and Orville Wright first arrived in 1900 — but not that much.

Kitty Hawk

The Indian name Kitty Hawk appeared on maps as early as 1738. The most popular version of the origin of the name is its reference to the Indian time of the hunting of the geese — "Killy Honk."

To most Americans Kitty Hawk, because of its place in world history, is the best known name associated with the Outer Banks. Although the flight of the Wright Brothers took place in the neighboring community of Kill Devil Hills, it was from the Kitty Hawk Weather Station that Orville Wright telegraphed home the news of their success. Consequently, when the newspapers ran the story, they printed as their dateline "Kitty Hawk" assuming it was the place where the first flight occurred.

There are delightful insights of conditions existing at Kitty Hawk at the turn of the century as expressed by Orville Wright in letters to his sister. Following are some of them:

Kitty Hawk is a fishing village. The people make what little living they have in fishing. They ship tons & tons of fish away every year to Baltimore and other northern cities, yet like might be expected in a fishing village, the only meat they ever eat is fish flesh, and they never have any of that. You can buy fish in Dayton at any time, summer or winter, rain or shine; but you can't here. About the only way to get fish is to go and catch them yourself. It is just like in the north, where our carpenters never have their house completed, nor painters their houses painted; the fishermen never has any fish.

But the sand! The sand is the greatest thing in Kitty Hawk and soon will be the only thing.

The sunsets here are the prettiest I have ever seen. The clouds light up with all colors, in the background, with deep blue clouds of various shapes fringed with gold before.

. . . There is no store in Kitty Hawk; that is not anything you would call a store. Our pantry in its most depleted state would be a mammoth affair compared with our Kitty Hawk stores . . .

On discussing experiments with the flying machine:

. . . We tried it with a tail in front, behind and every other way. When we got through, Will was so mixed up he couldn't even theorize. It has been with considerable effort that I have succeeded him in the flying business at all. He likes to chase buzzards, thinking they are eagles, and chicken hawks much better . . .

Kill Devil Hills

There are numerous stories of the origin of the name Kill Devil Hills. The most popular is that it is named after a brand of rum called "Kill Devil" that washed ashore from a shipwreck in early colonial days.

The Moment That Changed The Course Of History

North Carolina Archives

— 4 —

With the dawn of 20th century America, the Outer Banks was witness to one of mankind's most dramatic and far reaching events. Here near the base of a sandy mound called Kill Devil Hill, Orville and Wilbur Wright made the first successful flight in a heavier-than-air machine. By applying brilliant insight and engineering genius to flight research, the Wright Brothers fulfilled the dream of centuries. The time was 10:35 A. M., December 17, 1903. The world would never again be the same.

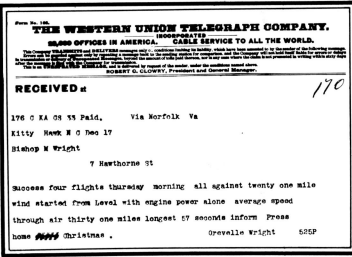

Orville Wright, 32, is at the controls as brother Wilbur, 36, looks on. The plane traveled 123 feet in 12 seconds. This photograph was taken by J. T. Daniels, a crew member of the Kitty Hawk Life-Saving Station, after Wilbur had set up the camera.

From The Wright Brothers Photo Collection

Surf at Kitty Hawk, 1900.

Machine on track, Big Kill Devil Hill, prior to December 14, 1903.

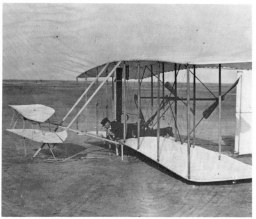

Wilbur Wright in damaged machine after unsuccessful trial of December 14, 1903.

Starting Orville in glider off Kill Devil Hill, 1902

Kitty Hawk Bay from 1900 camp.

Photos: National Park Service

Wilbur Wright in Kill Devil Hills Camp, August 29, 1902 (1901 glider).

Kitchen at Kitty Hawk, 1902.

Wilbur and Orville Wright on home porch (Dayton, Ohio) in 1911.   **Photos: National Park Service**

Looking toward the sound on November 12, 1932, the day the Wright Memorial was dedicated. Designed as a lighthouse, but never used for that purpose, the monument was constructed of gray-granite from Mt. Airy, North Carolina. It stands 61 feet above the summit of 90-foot Kill Devil Hill, a stabilized sand dune from which the Wright Brothers experimented with gliders in 1901-1902.

A U. S. air power tribute to Wilbur and Orville Wright on December 21, 1937.

Transporting the belongings of summer residents from pier to hotel on the Grand Trunk Railway.

Nags Head

Nags Head, according to the most oft-repeated tale, was named from the practice of land-based pirates who walked a horse on the beach at night with a lantern hanging from its neck. It was hoped that ships at sea would mistake the bobbing light for a ship closer to shore. The captain, believing it safe to change course, would run aground on the treacherous shoals — thus becoming easy prey for the pirates next day. It is interesting to note that Congress in 1825 passed a law deeming it a felony for anyone to show a light with the intention of confusing ships at sea into "danger or distress or shipwreck."

Regardless of how its name was derived, Nags Head from its early beginning was destined as a resort community for "sea bathing." By 1830 it could boast a hotel with accommodations for 200 guests; room and board for a month averaged 75 cents a day. Because the hotel was on the sound side, an 800-foot railway was built to take guests to and from the beach "for bathing and other purposes." Horses first pulled the cars; later oxen were used.

Eyeing the Prey

Library of Congress

Springing the Trap

Library of Congress

In 1851 a writer described Nags head as where

. . . intelligent and wealthy Carolinians regularly congregate about the first of July to pass in social intercourse surrounded by the health reviving breezes of the Old Ocean, the season of the year that would spare them to sickness on their plantations.

"Fashionables" stroll on the beach at Old Nags Head. Note the hotel nestled in the sand dunes. Having served as headquarters for General Henry A. Wise, CSA, the retreating Confederates burned this landmark when Union troops captured the Outer Banks in February, 1862.

From the 1890's to 1912, the *Neuse* sailed regularly between Elizabeth City and New Bern with stops at Roanoke Island. Following the Civil War and before the three-mile Wright Memorial Bridge was completed in 1930, the steam packet was the principal means of transportation to and from the Banks. There were times at ebb tide when early automobiles used the hard-packed sand at ocean's edge to travel to Norfolk and beyond.

This excursion boat made regular trips between Nags Head and Beaufort in the 1920's and the early 1930's.

Vacationers arriving at Old Nags Head Pier on a summer's day in the *Gay Nineties.*

Before the Old Nags Head Pier was constructed, passengers to Nags Head had to disembark on the west side of Roanoke Island, travel overland to Manteo from where they would board a sailing vessel for the short trip to Nags Head.

The hotel was the center of evening social activity where dancing was the featured attraction. Other than sun, surf and sand on a rugged windswept landscape, Nags Head offered few diversions. But that was enough, as here was a special place isolated from the rest of the world, where those with means could relax in easy surroundings and enjoy themselves unaffected by pretense and formality.

What mattered was good conversation, easy laughter and impeccable manners; where families enjoyed being together; and hospitality was lavish. It was a marvelous time in a splendid place, and for those that it touched the summers of Old Nags Head would forever glow in memory.

The seashore is the essence of total sensuous fulfillment. Now, as then, it continuously lures us back with warm memories of beach parties, sunset strolls and summer loves.

Young "fashionables" on the beach at Nags Head in the 1890's.

Spend Your Vacation at Nags Head and Roanoke Island

SEASHORE BATHING, BOATING and FISHING

GET really acquainted with this remarkable section of your own state, with its enchanting waters, its rich history, its hospitable and interesting people. Only 45 miles from Elizabeth City, in the heart of the wildfowl and fishing country where ocean breezes blow. Bathing, boating, and fishing for drumfish and ocean trout, that weigh 20 to 60 pounds apiece. See its picturesque and historical scenery, where the first English colonists landed nearly 400 years ago, and built the cradle of American history. Visit the lighthouses, the Coast Guard Stations, and the towering sand hills where the first airplane was made.

Take your car down. Nowhere can you have so good a time for so little money. Nowhere, will you find less noise, confusion and hustle that takes away the joy of vacations in other places. Reduced rates in effect on railroads and steamers.

These Comfortable Steamers Will Take You There:

Steamer ANNIE L. VAN SCIVER
Of the North River Line

Excursions every Sunday until September 12 inclusive, to Nags Head direct. Large Swift and Comfortable vessel. Leaves Elizabeth City 8 a. m. Returning leaves Nags Head at 5 p. m. arriving at 9:30 p. m. Low round trip fares. For further information address:

C. H. BROCK, Supt.
Elizabeth City, N. C.

Str. TRENTON
of Eastern Carolina Transportation Company

Capt. Martin Johnson, Master

Operating daily between Elizabeth City, Nags Head and Manteo. Leaves Eliz. City at 1:30 p. m. daily except Sunday, for Nags Head and Manteo. Returning leaves Manteo at 5 a. m. and Nags Head at 5:30 a. m. Meals on Boat and Automobile Accommodations.

Wanchese Line
Operating the Steamers:

HATTIE CREEF, POMPANO and O. T. & LLOYD, JR.

To Wanchese on Roanoke Island, Manns Harbor; Stumpy Point except Saturday. Steamers leave Elizabeth City at 12:30 daily. Automobile accommodations, at reduced round trip rates. For further information address

R. E. BLACK, Agt.
Elizabeth City, N. C.

An advertisement from the *Elizabeth City Independent* as printed in Catherine Bishir's *"The Unpainted Aristocracy:" The Beach Cottages of Old Nags Head.*

Fred Fearing Collection

The *Hattie Creef,* originally built as a sailing vessel, carried the Wright Brothers from Elizabeth City to Kitty Hawk. In 1904, the *Hattie Creef* was converted to a steamer and until the late 1930's, she continued on regular runs between Nags Head, Wanchese and Elizabeth CIty.

Fred Fearing Collection

A famous Nags Head excursion steamer, *Annie L. Vansciver* (shown here in the early 1900's), regularly left Elizabeth City in the morning and returned that evening. Black musicians, who entertained aboard with bones, bass fiddle and kazoo, made the ship especially popular.

— 19 —

National Archives

U. S. Coast Guard demonstration at the Nags Head Life Saving Station, 1949.

Jennette's Pier at Whalebone Junction in the 1940's.

Whalebone Junction, crossroads of the Outer Banks, is near the former site of Roanoke Inlet. The inlet served as the principal waterway for early colonists including those of the ill-fated colony on Roanoke Island whose leader, Captain John White, recorded it as being eleven to fifteen feet deep. In 1736 it was recorded as six feet deep and in 1783 only a foot deep having shifted south nearly a mile from where it was 200 years before. By the beginning of the 19th century the shifting sands of the Outer Banks had reclaimed the inlet.

A nifty summer cottage on the sound at Old Nags Head near the site of the ante-bellum hotel (see page 14).

— 21 —

"The manner of makinge their boates."

"The brovvyllinge of their fifhe"

Roanoke Indians as sketched by John White.

Roanoke Island

Roanoke Island is the site of the only Elizabethan colony in North America. From 1584 to 1590 Sir Walter Raleigh and Queen Elizabeth I made two attempts to establish a permanent English colony on Roanoke Island. Even though Raleigh's colonies were short-lived, he is remembered as the Father of English America. The dreams of Raleigh and his Queen to establish an English Empire in the New World were realized some 20 years later at Jamestown, Virginia.

Raleigh's second attempt at colonization on Roanoke Island in 1587 was under the direction of artist-Governor John White and seemed at first to be progressing well. In August of 1587, White's daughter gave birth to Virginia Dare, the first child of English parentage born in America.

A week after this happy event, Governor White returned to England for supplies and to recruit additional colonists. He left behind 112 people including his daughter and granddaughter. White was unable to return immediately because of hostilities with the Spanish. Upon his return to Roanoke Island in 1590, the colony had vanished; the only remaining traces were pieces of broken armour and the word "Croatoan" (an Indian tribe) carved on a tree. There are many theories as to what happened to the Lost Colony of Roanoke Island, but historians have not been able to verify any of them.

Artist's concept of John White's only link to his "lost colony"   North Carolina Archives

"Their manner of careynge ther Childern"

Throughout the latter part of the 17th century, settlers were increasingly attracted to the lush grazing lands of the area. As the land was gradually claimed by the newcomers, the Indians struck back in 1713 and in an attack that centered on Roanoke Island killed 40 settlers. It was the final act of desperation by a proud people.

* * * * *

During the Civil War a strong Union force, consisting of 80 vessels carrying 11,500 officers and men, approached Roanoke Island by way of Hatteras Inlet. Under the command of General Ambrose E. Burnside, they subdued, in short order, the 5,000 ill-equipped Confederate defenders. The fall of Roanoke Island, February 1862, insured Union control of the Outer Banks for the duration of the war.

Increasing numbers of runaway slaves, seeking the protection of the Union banner, began arriving on Roanoke Island soon after its capture. To cope with this, the Federal Government established an experimental colony on un-occupied land near present-day Manteo.

Streets were laid out and named and acre lots were plotted. By 1865 the colony had more than 3000 people living in nearly 600 cabins and huts.

But with the end of the war, the colony was disbanded when it was decided to return the land to the original owners. Some of the newly freed blacks remained in the area or relocated elsewhere along the Banks; most, however, returned to the mainland where there were better employment opportunities.

The Lost Colony, first presented here in 1937 to mark the 350th anniversary of the birth of Virginia Dare, is America's longest playing symphonic drama and is presented each summer at Waterside Theatre near the site of reconstructed Fort Raleigh.

A vacation on the Outer Banks would be incomplete without a visit to the North Carolina Marine Resources Center two miles north of Manteo on Highway 64. The center features a fine aquarium and museum and offers a wide variety of educational programs designed especially for children. Here, also, is the grave of Richard Etheridge, the highly respected black officer who for twenty years commanded Pea Island Life Saving Station (see page 42).

Commercial fishing off the Outer Banks in the 1930's.

For about 75 years, beginning shortly after the Civil War, commercial fishing for mullet, shad and herring was a way of life on the Outer Banks.

Chief Wanchese, **a modern ocean-going vessel, in home port.**

The working Fisherman's Wharf of Wanchese is as different — and certainly as interesting — as the famous one in San Francisco.

The art of shipbuilding continues in Wanchese.

President Franklin Roosevelt visits Roanoke Island on August 18, 1937, for the celebration of the 350th anniversary of the birth of Virginia Dare. Seated next to the President, in his special Pierce Arrow touring car, is North Carolina Congressman Warren Lindsay.

President Roosevelt, philatelist, suggested with this rough sketch the illustration of the Virginia Dare five-cent commemorative stamp, first issued at Manteo on August 18, 1937.

Fred Fearing Collection

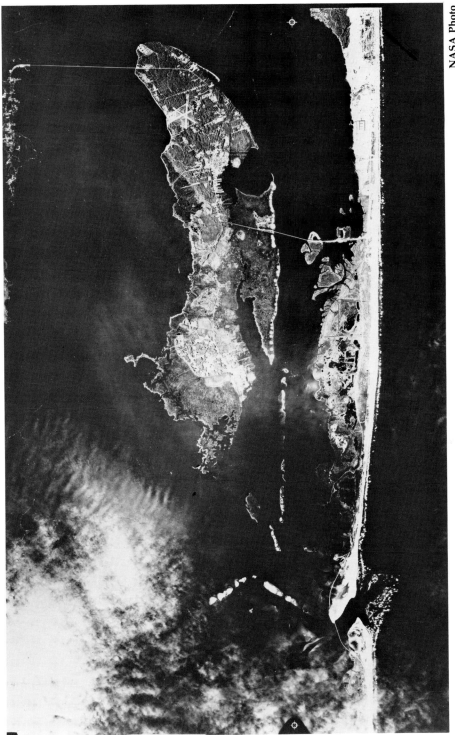

Roanoke Island From 12 Miles Up.

Roanoke Island is about seven miles long and two miles wide. Manteo and Wanchese, the island's two communities, were named by the post office to honor Indians befriended by the Raleigh colonists. The town of Manteo was formed in 1873 when the area was selected for the county seat of Dare County. Wanchese, known as *The Lower End* before 1886 when a post office was established there, is a thriving center for commercial fishing.

Cape Hatteras

On the Outer Banks, the highly renowned National Park Service manages Cape Hatteras National Seashore, as well as Wright Brothers National Memorial and Fort Raleigh National Historic Site. Administrative offices for the complex are located at Fort Raleigh on Roanoke Island.

First appearing on the Banks in 1933, the National Park Service assumed administration of the Wright Brothers Memorial from the War Department. In 1941 the Park Service was granted jurisdiction of Fort Raleigh on Roanoke Island by the state of North Carolina. The fort was reconstructed and the site designated Fort Raleigh National Historic Site.

Sea oats, tall grasses that have panicles resembling those of oats, thrive on exposed sandy shores. It was widely planted on the Outer Banks to bind sandy slopes.

National Seashore

After conducting a survey of America's unspoiled coastlines in 1937, the National Park Service recommended the establishment of Cape Hatteras National Seashore. But lack of funds, World War II and the possibility of oil under the Outer Banks combined to delay the establishment of the national seashore.

In 1952 the two children of Andrew Mellon donated $618,000 for land purchases of the Outer Banks with the condition that the state of North Carolina match the grant. The state quickly responded and by 1953 Cape Hatteras National Seashore, America's first, became a reality.

Bodie Island

The origin of the name Bodie (pronounced body) Island is uncertain, although indications are that it came from a family who were the island's first white inhabitants.

As with other areas of the Outer Banks, the forces of nature have constantly changed Bodie Island so that today it is no longer an island. As an island it extended from Roanoke Inlet in the north to an inlet at Rodanthe in the south. Since the 17th century, inlets have opened and closed at least six different times in this area.

Bodie Island has been the home of three lighthouses, two lifesaving stations and several large gun clubs. Since 1953 the National Park Service has administered a Natural History Museum at the old lighthouse keeper's quarters and a recreational area at Coquina Beach where during the summer months Life Saving Service rescue methods are demonstrated. A National Park Service concessioner operates the Oregon Inlet Fishing Center, the largest sports fisheries center on the Banks.

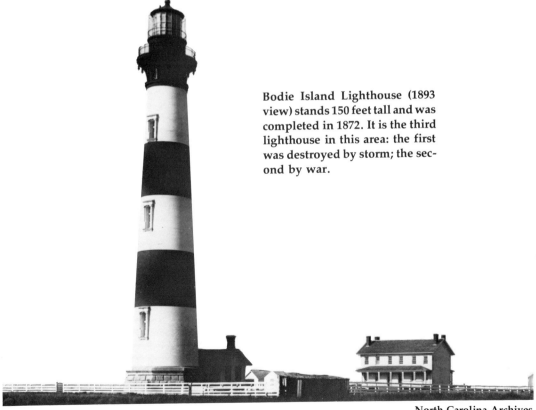

Bodie Island Lighthouse (1893 view) stands 150 feet tall and was completed in 1872. It is the third lighthouse in this area: the first was destroyed by storm; the second by war.

North Carolina Archives

The Herbert C. Bonner Bridge across Oregon Inlet was opened in 1963 and named to honor a U. S. Congressman from North Carolina.

Preparing to cross Oregon Inlet on a November day in 1934. Ferry service started here in 1924 and was under private ownership until 1941 when the state of North Carolina took it over.

U. S. Fish & Wildlife Service

Miss Oregon Inlet **returning to home port after a half-day fishing trip. Fishing boats are also available at Hatteras Village and on Roanoke Island.**

Life on the Outer Banks when

the World was a Little Younger

Pea Island National

Beginning at Oregon Inlet and for the next twelve miles south, Hatteras Island is set aside for the care and protection of wildlife, especially migratory waterfowl. Dedicated men and women of the highly respected U. S. Fish and Wildlife Service administer Pea Island National Wildlife Refuge.

In the course of a year, more than 265 species of birds can be seen on the refuge. Among the largest and most interesting are Canadian geese and snow geese that by the thousands make Pea Island their home, especially from September to May. Rarely are any seen during the summer months.

The four-mile trail around North Pond and the observation decks on the pond's dike afford excellent means to observe, study and photograph the exciting world of nature's wild.

Pea Island, named for the wild pea vine that grows there in abundance, was formed from Bodie Island when Oregon Inlet was opened in 1846. And like Bodie Island it is no longer an island, becoming part of larger Hatteras Island in 1922 when the inlet that formed its southern boundary was closed by the shifting sands of the Outer Banks.

Pea Island National Wildlife Refuge was established in 1938 after the Federal Government acquired the land mostly from private hunting clubs. Today the refuge covers 5,915 acres of the Outer Banks in addition to 25,700 acres of Pamlico Sound that are off limits to hunters.

A one day's bag, Goosewing Hunting Club, Outer Banks, NC, c. 1930.

Wildlife Refuge

U. S. Fish and Wildlife Service

Thousands of snow geese migrate to Pea Island each fall where they alight and enjoy themselves throughout the winter.

The attractive bayberry grows in profusion on the Outer Banks. Its rugged beauty and ability to survive in all kinds of soil and situations are matched only by its delicate fragrance. In colonial times wax was extracted from its berries and used for candles.

Across from the headquarters of Pea Island National Wildlife Refuge is the site of the old Pea Island Life Saving Station. It was established in 1878 and at the time of its closing in 1947, it had become the home of the nation's only black lifesaving crew. This station was regarded as one of the most effective and the men among the most daring of the United States Life Saving Service.

Captain Richard Etheridge (left) and his all-black crew of the Pea Island Life Saving Station, c. 1898.

The pride of the U. S. Coast Guard is reflected in these men of Pea Island Coast Guard Station, c. 1940. The Life Saving Service was joined with the Revenue Cutter Service in 1915 to form the U. S. Coast Guard.

U. S. Fish and Wildlife Service

Chicamacomico

Rodanthe, Waves, and Salvo — all post office names — were once part of the area known by the more enchanting Indian name, Chicamacomico. Here north of Rodanthe on the ocean side is Chicamacomico Life Saving Station, the best remaining example of the twelve stations that for nearly 75 years dominated the Outer Banks.

It all began in 1873 when Congress established the United States Life Saving Service. Its mission: to patrol the beaches looking for ships in distress and, thereupon, to take whatever action required to save human life.

The stations were located along the beach at seven-mile intervals — each had a crew of between five and ten men who patrolled on foot or horseback. They were mostly local men who were employed from December through March (later extended from September through April). But even when at home, the men were on call at any time in case of an emergency. The commander of the station was employed year-round.

It was from this station in 1918 that a courageous Coast Guard crew entered a sea of flames to rescue 47 of the 57-man crew of the torpedoed British tanker *Mirlo*. For this feat and disregard for their own lives, six men of the Chicamacomico Life Saving Station in 1921 received Gold Life Saving Medals from the British Government and in 1930 the Grand Crosses of the American Cross of Honor from the United States Government, a medal that has been awarded only eleven times.

Stop for a moment and stroll among these proud weathered buildings that for over 100 years have defiantly withstood the ravages of time and storm. Here, not very long ago, a hearty lot of good men lived and worked; here they laughed and argued; here they shared good times and tales of heroic deeds.

Returning home to their families after a tour of duty, they were ready in a moment's notice to risk their lives so that others might live and be saved from the perils of the sea. This was their legacy — a legacy that continues to this day in the proud tradition of the U. S. Coast Guard.

Chicamacomico Life Saving Coast Guard Station in 1951, three years before it was closed by the Coast Guard. This station is the only one of the original twelve between Kitty Hawk and Ocracoke that remains intact on its original site.

Launching the surf boat, c. 1900. Surf boats were used when an endangered vessel was beyond range of a shot-line. The line was fired from shore to ship, whereupon seamen in distress would swing ashore in breeches buoy or life cars.

U. S. Coast Guard demonstration at Nags Head Life Saving Station on May 21, 1949. Today three U. S. Coast Guard stations carry on the job of saving lives and property along the Hatteras coast.

Using a breeches buoy, the Coast Guard rescues a crewman from the wrecked schooner, *W. N. Reinhardt, June 8, 1927.*

Chicamacomico Races

During the Civil War a fascinating encounter occurred here. After the Confederate forts at Hatteras Inlet fell, the Union commander there dispatched a 600-man column north to Chicamacomico to thwart any possibility of a Confederate advance down the beach.

On learning of this force and assuming it was directed against their positions on Roanoke Island, the Confederates, in turn, sent a Georgia regiment to Chicamacomico to bring on an engagement. In an amphibious assault, part of the Georgia troops came ashore on the sound side while the remaining stayed aboard ship and continued southward.

The Union forces, upon realizing the Confederate plan to encircle them, immediately took off down the beach for Cape Hatteras — 25 miles south. A forced march through loose sand with the sun beating down was difficult enough. But with Georgia troops in close pursuit, the fear of entrapment at any moment and without water, it was, by all accounts, hell itself for the Union forces.

Near midnight the weary troops finally reached the old Cape Hatteras Lighthouse and fresh water. The Georgians, in the meantime, camped on the beach between the lighthouse and Kinnakeet (Avon).

Union reinforcements arrived next morning and without danger of being cut off (Confederate vessels were unable to execute a landing), Union troops once again headed north along the beach. The Confederates retreated. From the ocean side, a Union warship appeared and shelled the retreating column without effect.

There was no further encounter; both sides wearily returned to their camps. But for the men involved, there would be no forgetting what history came to record as the Chicamacomico Races.

North Carolina Archives

Exhausted men of the 20th Indiana Infantry bivouacked at Cape Hatteras on the night of October 4, 1861, after their retreat from Chicamacomico.

Kinnakeet

A Place Deserving of Discovery

Kinnakeet Inlet, site of a once-thriving shipbuilding industry, is today barely a shadow of its former self. Turn off at the water tower and experience a place of time past where magnificent forests once flourished.

Kinnakeet — another fine Indian name for a place now called Avon after a post office was established there in 1873 — was once the center of a heavily wooded area of magnificent oaks and cedars. Those trees extended nearly 40 miles along the Banks. The live oak was of such quality that it was used in the construction of America's proud clipper ships.

Because of this resource, a ship-building industry developed here before the Civil War and Kinnakeet soon became known for its fine schooners. But man's indiscriminate cutting of trees on the delicate landscape led to the appearance of sand dunes where once thick forests stood. Growing in size the dunes soon took over, covering the remaining trees and eventually destroying two small communities along with Kinnakeet's ship-building industry.

Today there is little to indicate what once was; nature has never fully recovered. It was perhaps America's first example of what can happen when, because of man's greed, the land is abused and mistreated. Unfortunately, there is little to indicate that anyone ever noticed.

Looking westward across the expanse of Pamlico Sound as you approach Cape Hatteras is the longest distance between the Banks and the western mainland. Could this be Verrazzano's Sea, the place where Giovanni da Verrazzano, an Italian in the service of the French, declared that he had discovered the passage to the East? Da Verrazzano made the first recorded European visit to the Outer Banks in 1524; and for more than a hundred years afterwards explorers searched for the body of water known as Verrazzano's Sea.

North Carolina State Archives

Two-masted schooners of the type built at Kinnakeet, tied up at Elizabeth City, NC, c. 1895.

Cape Hatteras

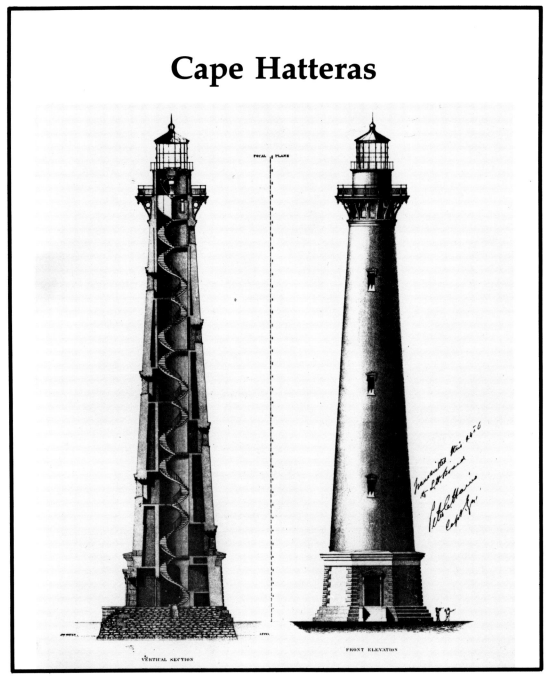

VERTICAL SECTION   FRONT ELEVATION

An 1869 print of the lighthouse proposed for Cape Hatteras. Completed in 1871, it was at the time of its construction the tallest lighthouse in North America standing 191 feet above the main high water mark with 268 steps to reach its light. Although constantly threatened by the sea, it is still in service.

Cape Hatteras Lighthouse has two 1,000-watt rotating lamps each yielding a beacon of 800,000 candlepower. At a distance it appears as a short flash every 7½ seconds and is visible in clear weather about 20 miles distant — although it has been observed 50 miles at sea. This photograph was taken about 1895. Note to the right of the keeper's house the ruins of the original lighthouse built in 1802 and dismantled after the Civil War. See page 47 for a drawing of this earlier lighthouse.

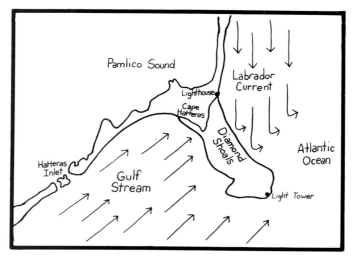

Diamond Shoals

The Outer Banks, since the early 16th century, has witnessed more than 650 shipwrecks, thus the name "Graveyard of the Atlantic." The reason is the Diamond Shoals — underwater sandbars that are about three miles wide and extend nine miles out from Cape Hatteras. They are kept relatively constant as they constitute the point where the warm waters of the Gulf Stream from the south collide with the cold waters of the Labrador Current from the north.

To warn ships of the Diamond Shoals, Congress in 1794 authorized a lighthouse at Cape Hatteras. Later lighthouses were constructed on Bodie Island and Ocracoke. To further minimize the danger, prior to the Civil War lightships were anchored on the edge of the shoals to be replaced in 1967 by a light tower that stands today warning ships at sea of the menacing Diamond Shoals.

Light tower on far edge of the Diamond Shoals that in 1967 replaced the lightship

The hurricane of 1837 devastated the North Carolina coast. Known as "Racer's Storm," it destroyed three ships off the Banks and took 90 lives. However, the worst maritime disaster in the annals of Outer Banks history occurred during the winter of 1877-78 when two steam ships were wrecked and 188 lives lost.

On November 24, 1877, the *USS Huron* in heavy seas ran aground on the beach at Nags Head (north of Jockey's Ridge) with 103 lives lost (see page 55). Two months later and thirty miles further south, the *Metropolis* wrecked with 85 lives lost.

Congress quickly reacted to these disasters and authorized additional lifesaving stations and personnel for the Banks. By the following year eleven new stations were built and operating.

University of North Carolina

The wrecked barkentine *Priscilla,* a victim of hurricane San Ciriaco which struck the Outer Banks on August 17, 1899. The ship's captain, Benjamin Springsteen, lost his wife and two sons in the storm, but he and nine crewmen were saved by the daring and herculean efforts of Rasmus Midgett of the U. S. Life Saving Service who later received the Gold Lifesaving Medal.

Lightship 69 was pulled from its mooring off the Diamond Shoals in August of 1899 and driven ashore by the force of Hurricane San Ciriaco's 120 mile an hour gusts. The nine crewmen aboard were saved and the ship was later refloated. Nineteen years later, in August 1918, a German submarine sank the ship's successor, *Lightship 71*, after she had radioed a nearby merchant ship of the submarine's position. The lightship's crew was allowed to abandon ship before the U-boat shelled and sank her.

A casualty of Hurricane San Ciriaco found on the beach near Hatteras in 1899. Of the thirteen vessels that happened to be off the Outer Banks when the storm struck, seven were wrecked on the beach, six disappeared without a trace and more than 59 lives were lost.

U. S. S. Huron,

LOST NOVEMBER 24TH, 1877, NEAR OREGON INLET, N. C.

Library of Congress

The *USS Huron* on a scientific cruise to Cuba encountered heavy weather and wrecked off Nags Head shortly after 1 a.m., November 24, 1877. For a time her crew worked to free the ship in what appeared to be little danger. But she soon keeled over, carrying 98 officers and men to their deaths. The lives of five others were claimed during subsequent salvage operations.

— 55 —

On May 3, 1929, the four-masted schooner, *A. Ernst Mills*, carrying a cargo of salt, sank off the Outer Banks with a loss of three lives. When the salt dissolved, the ship rose from the ocean depths. In the above photo a salvage crew prepares to tow her to shore.

Still exhibiting that certain majesty that only sailing ships possess, the four-masted schooner, *G. A. Kohler*, lies high and dry on the beach at Salvo in 1934. The Chicamacomico Coast Guard crew rescued the nine seamen aboard during the storm of August 1933. The vessel remained on the beach until World War II when it was burned for its scrap iron for use in the war effort.

National Park Service

On the sound side of Cape Hatteras is an attractive wooded area known as Buxton where the Hatteras Indians lived. On early maps and deeds the place is referred to as "Cape Hatteras Indian Town." Here is the site of Buxton Woods, the largest forest on the Outer Banks. Note the contrast in vegetation and climate from the area north of Cape Hatteras. This marked change is due to the influence of the warm Gulf Stream flowing from the south.

National Park Service

Rugged live oaks once grew in profusion on the Outer Banks and were used in shipbuilding. This photo was taken in 1934 in Hatteras Woods.

Nearby is the small community of Frisco that was named by the post office after the city of San Francisco. This village is the site of where the last Yaupon Tea, the famous Outer Banks brand of tea, was processed. Made from the abundant Yaupon holly plant, the tea was first used by Indians for medicinal purposes and before the American Revolution by the colonists as a patriotic substitute for British tea. It continued to be commercially produced in Frisco until the early 1900's.

The sinking of the *USS Monitor.*

In 1862 the Civil War ironclad *Monitor* sank in a fierce storm 16 miles southeast of Cape Hatteras. Under tow, she was bound for Beaufort, North Carolina and blockade duty along the Carolina coast. In 1975 the United States Government designated the area around the *Monitor* as the nation's first marine sanctuary, thereby protecting the submerged wreckage where she lies under 220 feet of water.

During the summer of 1983, the *Monitor's* 1300-pound anchor was recovered from the ocean floor and taken to East Carolina University to be preserved. The ship's hull will probably never be raised due to the irreparable damage it sustained during World War II. American warships, guided by sonor beeps, dropped tons of depth charges on what was thought to be a U-boat.

The *Monitor's* place in history was assured March 9, 1862, when for four hours she battled the Confederate ironclad, *Virginia* (originally named the *Merrimack*), at Hampton Roads, Virginia. While the clash ended inconclusively, it heralded the end of wooden warships and launched the era of the armored dreadnought.

General William (Billy) Mitchell in May 1920 by his plane (V.E. 7) marked with his personal insignia.

In September 1923, from an improvised airstrip near Hatteras Village, General Billy Mitchell's planes took off in an effort to sink two obsolete United States battleships anchored off the Diamond Shoals. It was a compelling demonstration of air power in modern warfare.

A Martin bomber pilot at Hatteras prior to Mitchell's bombing demonstration.

General William (Billy) Mitchell was born in 1879 in Nice, France and raised in Milwaukee, Wisconsin. He enlisted in the army early in the Spanish-American War, was soon commissioned and rose rapidly to become at 33 the youngest officer ever appointed to the General Staff. He became a superlative pilot and during World War I directed the massive Allied flight of 1481 planes against German lines. He returned home a highly decorated hero.

As the foremost champion of air power, Mitchell advocated a strong, separate air force, warned of growing Japanese military might and on three occasions (1921-1923) directed demonstrations that proved airplanes could sink battleships. Impatient with what he considered the lack of appreciation of the role air power was destined to play, Mitchell in 1925 charged the War Department and Navy Department with "incompetency, criminal negligence and treasonable administration of national defense." He was court-martialed for insubordination, found guilty and sentenced to a five year suspension from military service. He resigned his commission from the army in 1926. Ten years later he died in New York City.

In 1946 the United States Congress voted General Mitchell a special Medal of Honor — the nation's belated but grateful appreciation to a courageous and farsighted American.

Martin bombers (MB-2) of the Army Air Service were the type airplane used by General Billy Mitchell in his demonstrations to prove the airplane had greatly reduced the efficiency of the battleship.

Department of Defense

The obsolete battleship, *New Jersey*, about to be sunk in General Mitchell's demonstration off Cape Hatteras, September 1923.

The battleship, *Virginia*, badly damaged but still afloat, after Mitchell's initial attack. It took eight planes dropping thirteen 1,100 pound bombs to sink this once proud capital ship of the United States Navy.

At Hatteras Inlet were twin Confederate forts — Fort Hatteras and Fort Clark — that early in the war came under Union attack. No sooner had the Confederates completed construction of the forts in late August 1861, than a Union naval force of seven warships and three troopships appeared on the horizon. Over the next two days, in a joint army-navy operation the Union forces succeeded in capturing both Confederate forts. With this and the fall of Roanoke Island five months later, the Outer Banks fell under Union control that was never relinquished.

The shifting sands of the Outer Banks have concealed any remnants of the forts. When aboard the ferry, note how narrow the inlet is becoming. Like Roanoke Inlet at Nags Head, these sands may someday close this inlet and form a new one elsewhere on the Banks.

North Carolina Archives

Currier and Ives print of the bombardment of the forts at Hatteras Inlet, NC, August 1861 . . .

. . . and capture of the forts at Cape Hatteras Inlet; troops coming ashore through the surf, August 1861.

Impressions of Hatteras
in 1861

Shortly after the capture of Fort Hatteras and Fort Clark, a talented 18 year-old Union soldier, Charles F. Johnson of the 9th New York Volunteers (Hawkins Zouaves), arrived on Hatteras where he sketched in pen and described in detail the Hatteras scene as it appeared to him. Following are some of his sketches and descriptions taken from *The Long Role,* a book published in 1911 and based on his writings during his two year tour of duty (1861-1863) with the Union Army.

Tuesday, October 1st

Secured a pass yesterday and brought back seven sketches with me, chiefly little rural scenes which surprised me here and there during our ramble, with a strange musty sort of beauty, nestling under the low range of verdure barely visible from our camp.

. . . The houses are all dismal enough and are only saved from complete lack of interest by a certain mossy coat which forms on everything except the uncompromising sand, and lends a gray green tinge, which puts all things here from the hand of man, in harmony with Nature in a very short time. Wild grapes, larger and richer than many tame varieties in the North, are here in great abundance nourished as much, it would seem, by the salt sea breeze as by the juices pumped out of the sandy soil by the roots. Figs also grow here, but are not yet ripe.

Moonlight at Trent

Sunday, Dec. 1

Thain and I have spent a pleasant evening with Corporal Davis and Sergeant Johnson in their tent. Davis is our artist and possesses extra-ordinary genius for one so young . . . Davis gave me some instructions on my favorite pasttime. I need to show more decisive shading in my pencilings, make up objects stronger and in sharper relief. He was pleased with my moonlight scene from Trent (now Frisco), touched it up some and then made a small drawing for me from the idea it had furnished.

Camp Winfield
December 11

Duncan Creek

Companies A, B, C, H, and 'Ours' struck tents at Camp Wool this morning and we are now about a mile further up the Island, on a high sand knoll near Duncan Creek.

   . . . *Everything on the Island seems to be devoid of paint — dwellings, barns and windmills, of which there are a greater number than I supposed were in existence in the whole country.*

   . . . *These windmills, by the way, are about the only things picturesque on the Island, and as objects of study for an amateur artist they are admirable. I have sketches of them, I believe, from here to Chicamacomico, taken from all possible points of view, for they are all built after one plan.*

Wednesday, December 4

Yesterday I was on guard at the lower windmill near Company E's quarters back of our camp. The weather was extremely cold, damp and disagreeable during the day and night. This morning when the sun came up over the Atlantic warm and strong, the vapory mosses were soon rolled away in pleasant shapes, clouds which in hte distance took on warm and brilliant hues. I sketched the scene of our camp a little after sunrise, from a small square window near the roof of the mill, form which one has a birds-eye view of seven miles of Hatteras Bank and out over the Atlantic with Camp Wool in the foreground.

At this time in the morning, the scene is an animated one. The wharf is thronged with the fishermen selling fish to soldiers. Breakfast fires are smoking. Soldiers are at early drill, if they can't get out of it; bugles and drums sound their call and that; everywhere activity and life which produces a very pleasant impression after a cold night on guard with only shivery snatches of sleep in a rickety old windmill on Hatteras Bank.

Monday, Nov. 25th

Have just come in from another twenty-four-hour picket duty. This time on what is called the Church Picket, which is accounted one of the best to be on in cold weather, and yet I feel the effects of what little sleep I got. There seems to be something about this infernal sand – bank calculated for "chills and fever," for even in hot weather the sand is damp and cold and will chill through any frame that must recline on it.

Note – no date*

The Sketch of Hatteras at sundown from Camp Wool is about the essence of the last days of restrained impatience. The crooner scuddling (schooner sailing) homeward lightly on the waves, before a darkening sky; the sun sinking large and glorious in its splendor, dyeing the waves in wonderful hues; the huge gun booming over the brilliant waters, and while the white clouds yet curl upward, we say – "Farewell Hatteras."

*Johnson's unit at this time was preparing for the invasion of Roanoke Island and in keeping with military regulations of the time no date was mentioned although he indicated something was up with "Note — no date."

U. S. Weather Bureau Signal Station at Hatteras, c. 1904.

In 1870 Congress assigned the U. S. Signal Corps responsibility for a national weather service. Its mission: to take meterological observations for the purpose of weather forecasting and to issue warnings of severe storms and impending floods. Four years later, August 1874, a weather station was established on the Banks with the Cape Hatteras Lighthouse keeper's quarters serving as the station (see page 51). Since 1957 the Hatteras Weather Station, one of about 250 Weather Bureau offices and stations throughout the United States, has been in Buxton.

In the early 1900's the Outer Banks seemed to hold a particular fascination for inventors. While the Wright Brothers were experimenting off Kill Devil Hill, Reginald L. Fessenden, a special agent for the U. S. Weather Bureau from 1901-1903 and a former member of Thomas Edison's staff, made the first successful message transmission between 50-foot towers on Cape Hatteras and Roanoke Island. Even though Guglielmo Marconi has been credited with development of the wireless telegraph, Fessenden's discovery is credited as the basis for radio broadcasting.

North Carolina Archives

Awaiting the ferry, c. 1930.

. . . and 52 years later at Hatteras Inlet.

. . . Aboard the Ferry, c. 1930

The state of North Carolina has operated the Hatteras Ferry since 1954.

Ocracoke

Days of romance, pirates, excitement and adventure are all captured in the word and place called Ocracoke.

Legend has it that the name Ocracoke originated with the pirate, Blackbeard, who impatiently awaiting dawn to do battle with Lieutenant Robert Maynard, cried out "O crow cock! O crow cock!" Actually, however, maps charted before Blackbeard's time identify the place as "Wokokon," a name most likely of Indian origin.

Here the most feared and notorious pirate of them all, Blackbeard, sometimes made his home base. For over two years, with impunity, he ravaged the shipping lanes off the Carolina Banks — robbing, destroying and killing.

But it was the colony of Virginia that finally took him to task to "put a stop to ye further Progress of the Robberys." Two small sloops were outfitted, neither having armament nor guns. Their combined crews of 54 men were detailed from the British Navy.

North Carolina Archives

Under the command of Lieutenant Robert Maynard and equipped with only swords and small arms, this group of brave, determined men set sail. Their chances of defeating Blackbeard aboard his 8-gun ship, *Adventurer*, was anything but encouraging.

Late on November 21, 1718, they approached Ocracoke. With the arrival of dawn and with pistols and muskets at the ready, they attacked. Blackbeard responded with a devastating volley of cannonshot that disabled both attacking vessels. The smaller of the two, *Ranger*, was seriously damaged and forced out of action. Aboard the other vessel, Lieutenant Maynard ordered his men to lie low as they drifted helplessly toward the awaiting pirate ship that had run aground and was unable to maneuver.

Edward Teach, the man known as Blackbeard.

Completed in 1823, the 65-foot Ocracoke Lighthouse is the oldest along the North Carolina coast.

As the ships met, the pirates, led by Blackbeard, swarmed aboard for the kill. But the tough British, led by their young officer, rose up en masse and in a bloody hand to hand encounter overcame their attackers. Blackbeard received a severe gash on the side of his neck and numerous pistol shots before keeling over dead. Battle casualties were nine pirates killed and fifteen captured; the British suffered eight killed and eighteen wounded.

Lieutenant Maynard and his men triumphantly returned to Virginia with Blackbeard's head firmly secured to the ship's bow-sprit. The captured pirates were taken to Williamsburg where they were tried and, with one exception, hanged.

Due to its isolation, Ocracoke is among the few places in the United States that still retains an unspoiled vestige of its original charm and character. The only public transportation to the island is the state-owned ferry service.

Upon leaving the Hatteras Ferry, a ride on the lone highway to the village of Ocracoke will reveal long stretches of pristine, deserted beaches.

A visit to the village of Ocracoke with its unpaved side streets, picket fences, small family graveyards and nature's live oak, the Yaupon tea tree and semi-tropical bloom of mimosas, gardenias and oleander will leave memories that linger long after a visit. Adding to its charm are old summer cottages encircling lovely Silver Lake where pleasure and commercial vessels are moored along its docks. It is a place haunted by time passed where at any moment one almost expects an 18th century square rig to appear on the horizon.

For Ocracoke, if it is anything, is rare, fragile and historically precious. To visit there is to dream of a time that was and is no more, of long vanished men both good and bad.

National Park Service

The "wild ponies" of Ocracoke roamed freely before the building of the highway in 1957. For the safety of ponies and visitors, these descendants of shipwrecked Spanish mustangs are in pens on the sound side of the highway midway between the village of Ocracoke and the Hatteras Ferry landing.

The Joe Bell Legend

The Outer Banks teems with legends. As this historical adventure ends, we would like to recount one of the most poignant tales of this special place.

The daisy-like red and yellow gaillardia that abounds in wild clusters on the sands of the Outer Banks is one of the most beautiful and yet one of the hardiest wild flowers in the area. Its bloom opens in April and seldom fades before December. To the residents of Ocracoke, it is known as the Joe Bell flower.

Joe Bell was born to a family of distinction in Washington, North Carolina; but, to their chagrin, Joe fell in love with a woman who they felt was unworthy of the family's social standing. As the romance became more serious, Joe's family sent him to Europe on "pressing business;" upon his return Joe found his sweetheart had been persuaded to marry another.

Not bearing to live in the same town where his love lived with another and angry with himself for bowing to family pressure, Joe sought a place where he could live in isolation.

A heart-broken Joe Bell arrived in Ocracoke and immediately found the respect of the local residents who persuaded him to serve as magistrate because of his education and business experience. But try as hard as he might, Joe could not fulfill his duties; consequently, he became more and more of a recluse. He was often seen walking alone with bunches of the red and yellow flowers. The local folk, nevertheless, liked him and in a strange sort of way even respected him. They would leave baskets of food on his doorstep and upon returning for their baskets would find them full of gaillardias — Joe's token of thanks. One day Joe Bell was found dead in his fishing boat surrounded by freshly picked flowers that today bear his name. The memory of Joe Bell will linger on the Outer Banks as long as the gaillardia blooms on its shores.

The Joe Bell flower

Silver Lake, the harbor at Ocracoke, where

commerce and recreation nicely blend.

Graves of four British seamen whose ship was torpedoed by a U-boat during World War II. This small cemetery in Ocracoke is maintained by the U. S. Coast Guard and is certainly worthy of a visit.

Epilogue

After the successful flight in 1903, Orville Wright wrote:

Isn't it astonishing that all these secrets
have been preserved for so many years just so
we could discover them?

In a similar way it is our hope that this book may have been a source of discovery for you of some of the highlights that make up the rich legacy of the Outer Banks.

As stated in the beginning, this book is an outline of historic events — nothing more. It is designed to assist you to better understand and thereby to better enjoy your visit to this fascinating place. For an in-depth study of the topics covered, we suggest you visit the various National Park Service visitor centers, the Pea Island headquarters of the U. S. Fish and Wildlife Service, U. S. Coast Guard Stations and the North Carolina Marine Resources Center. For a more complete and interesting account of the history of the Outer Banks, we recommend David Stick's *The Outer Banks.*

Farewell

For Further Reading

Edwin C. Bearss, *Rescue Operations from Chicamacomico Station 1874-1954.* National Park Service, September, 1965.

Catherine W. Bishir, *"The Unpainted Aristocracy:" The Beach Cottages of Old Nags Head.* North Carolina Department of Cultural Resources, Division of Archives and History, 1980.

E. C. Bruce, "Loungings in the Footprints of the Pioneers," *Harper's New Monthly Magazine,* XX (May, 1860), p. 729.

Francis Ross Holland, *America's Lighthouses: their illustrated history since 1716.* Stephen Green Press, Brattleboro, Vermont, 1972.

Charles F. Johnson, *The Long Role,* 1911.

Donald and Carol McAdoo, *Reflections of the Outer Banks.* Island Publishing House, Manteo, North Carolina, 1976.

Helen Hunt Miller, *Historic Places Around the Outer Banks.*

Edward R. Outlaw, Jr., *Old Nag's Head.* Liskey Lithograph Corp., Norfolk, Virginia, 1956.

David Stick, *Graveyard of the Atlantic.* University of North Carolina Press, Chapel Hill, 1952.

_____ *The Outer Banks Of North Carolina.* University of North Carolina Press, Chapel Hill, 1958.

Centerfold:
 Yacht on Outer Banks, c. 1932
 Beach scene, 1898
 Car on wooden tracks, 1930's
 Pea Island Coast Guard Station, c. 1940
 Windmill, 1907
 Oregon Inlet Ferry, 1930's
 Kinakeet Life Saving Station c. 1890's
 Fishermen at Manteo, 1905
 Cape Hatteras Lighthouse

Acknowledgments

This guide is the result of many people who have assisted in the research. We gratefully acknowledge the assistance of Richard Lankford and Kim Wade, North Carolina Division of Archives and History; James Trimble and James Delaney, National Archives; Captain A. D. Super, U. S. Coast Guard; the audio-visual staff, Department of Defense; the National Park Service staff, Cape Hatteras National Seashore; Ruthanne Heriot and Bruce Hopkins, National Park Service Interpretative Design Center; Donnie Browning and Beverly Midgett, Pea Island National Wildlife Refuge; and Jerry Cotten, University of North Carolina. Special thanks is extended to Edwin C. Bearss, Chief Historian National Park Service, for his review of the manuscript and to Fred Fearing and David Stick for making their photo collections available to us.

Index

T

Teach, Edward, ill. 74
Trent, 67

U

U-Boat, 54, 59, 80
Union Army, vi, 14, 24, 47, 64, 66
U.S. Fish and Wildlife Service, 40, 81

V

Verrazzano, Giovanni da, 49
Virginia (CSA), 59
Virginia, ill. 63
Virginia, 74, 76

W

W.N. Reinhardt, ill. 46
Wanchese, 20, 19, 27, 31
Waterside Theatre, ill. 25
Waves, 43
Weather Bureau, 71
Weather Station, 2, ill. 71
Whalebone Junction, 21
White, John, 21-22, ill. 23-24
Williamsburg, 76
Windmill, ill. 39
Wise, Henry A., 14
Wokokon, 74
World War I, 61
World War II, 59, 80
Wright Brothers, 2-3, 5, ill. 6, ill. 8-11, 19, 71, 81
    National Memorial, 32
Wright Memorial, ill. 10
Wright Memorial Bridge, 15

Y

Yaupon Tea, 58, 76

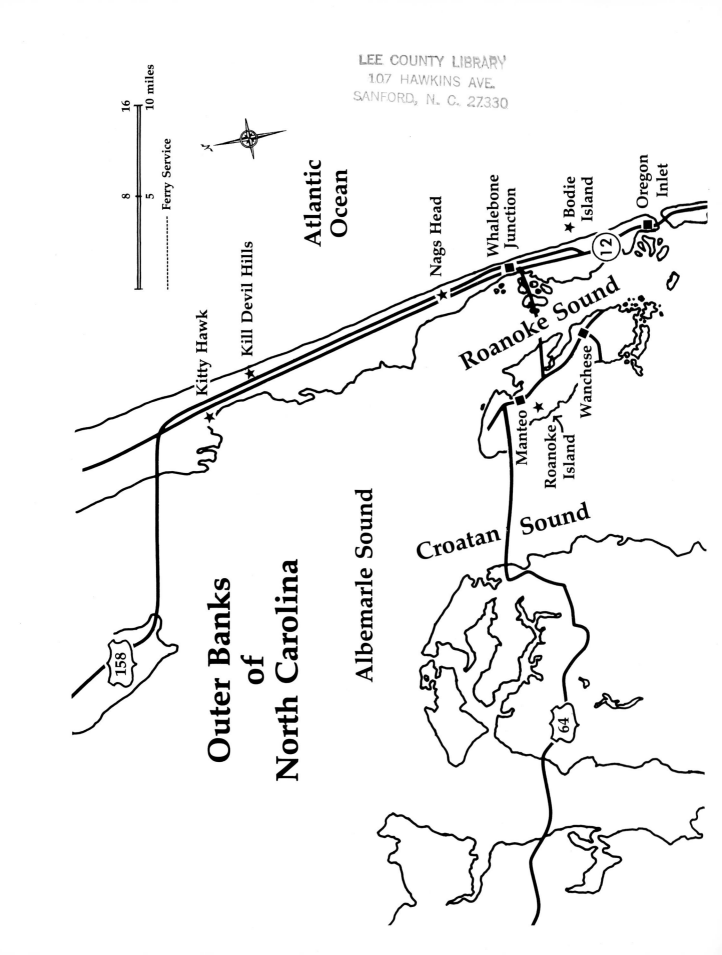

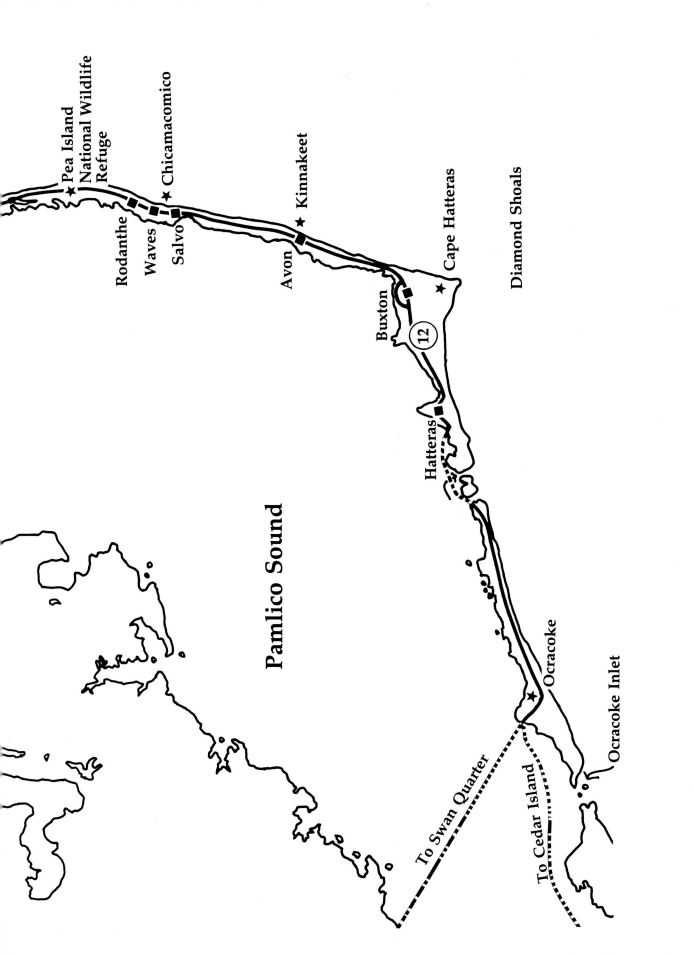

This book is set in
12 point Palatino typeface,
printed by
Specialty Binding and Printing
Shepherdstown, West Virginia
on 80 lb. Warren Lustro Coated Dull.
1984